WRESTLING COBRA

ASH JACKSON

WRESTLING COBRA

MY TIME AS AN AUSSIE WRESTLER

Ingram Spark

Also Available from the Author:
"BEYOND TRANS"
ISBN: 9780975654613

Discover the riveting life journey of Ash Jackson, an award-winning musician who turned her pain into powerful music. From her childhood dreams of fame, struggles with self-esteem, and experiences of bullying, to her pro wrestling career, battles with mental health, and remarkable courage in navigating her gender affirmation, her story is one of resilience, self⬦discovery, and redemption. Ash's music is more than an expression of art; it is a raw portrayal of her life, encapsulating themes of loneliness, love, and trauma. Yet, Ash's life is not solely confined to the realm of music. Her involvement in the anti-lockdown movement in Melbourne, and her subsequent defection and fallout are just some episodes of her multifaceted tale

Further information can be found at.
www.ashjackson.com

Copyright © 2024 by Ash Jackson

All rights reserved. No part of this book may be reproduced in any manner whatsoever without written permission except in the case of brief quotations embodied in critical articles and reviews.

First Printing, 2024

FOREWORD BY MATTHEW MUIR "JUNGLE CAT"

I first met Ash back in late 1999. I'd just made my debut as a Professional Wrestler. As someone who had represented Australia in both bodybuilding and powerlifting, I thought Professional Wrestling was going to be a breeze and I'd pick it up quickly. In short: it wasn't and I didn't. Pro Wrestling was VERY MUCH harder than I thought it would ever be. But I digress. I'd heard a lot about a Victorian Wrestler called "Cobra". Tough. Skilled. Had to be seen to be believed. Pro Wrestlers are not known for "putting over" (praising) their fellow workers and it was high praise indeed that I was hearing. All the talk was right.

I remember vividly a match at the Macedonian Club in Epping where Ash (as Cobra) and Ricky Diamond brought the house down. The capacity crowd on their feet screaming at the conclusion. The wrestler's change rooms were a "curtain sell out". All of the wrestlers watched the match, as best they could from whatever position they could find backstage, and I can remember thinking to myself "There's no way I'll EVER reach THAT level...". Both disappointed in my own shortcomings and stunned at the level of athleticism I had just witnessed, I joined a standing ovation that all of the wrestlers gave both Ash and Ricky as they entered the change room. Ricky was covered in blood and Ash was being carried by a security guard on each side supporting the spent athlete who had just torn the house down. Stunned I looked at Ash... his eyes rolled back into his head. And he collapsed to the floor. A collective gasp went up from ALL the wrestlers... Then Ash stood bolt upright. HUGE smile on his face. And said: "GOTCHA!". We all laughed and took turns coming over to shake Ash's hand. Still the best match I've ever seen live.

Fast forward a dozen or so years and we're in the age of social media. I'm scrolling Facebook one day and the name "Ash Jackson" comes up as a profile. Whether it was me requesting friendship or Ash I honestly can't remember. Either way, we pick right up where we left off, with Ash openly and candidly talking about her transition. After many years of partying and working security within the LGBT community, I'm nowadays described as an ally.

I've always felt protective and supportive of people that we're marginalised. And had the highest respect for people who have fought through adversity. This describes many of my trans friends and certainly describes Ash.

She has put her journey and struggle into the public eye for all to see. Her candor was disarming and raised her even further esteem of her character...

We ALL face struggles in our lives. Some face it quietly and some stoically...others like myself turn to self-medication and self-loathing. During a very low patch in my life (just a few years ago) I was at my wits end. Not sure what to do or where to turn and finding myself consumed with self-destructive thoughts I'd never seriously entertained before, I reached out to quite a few people I considered close to me with none returning my communication, except Ash... Her messages were thoughtful and considerate. Showing that over the previous few years, she'd TRULY listened to me and valued me at a level where she'd thought of what could give me hope and ease my mind. All were contained in quickly returned messages and an open invitation to come to Melbourne and stay with her until things got better. I was humbled to the point of silence and honestly moved to tears.

Despite her own struggles and personal demons she still hadn't lost that love or loyalty for her friends. I felt the same way again being asked to write this foreword: Humbled that Ash would ask me. I've always admired her for many different reasons. I'm looking forward to fully reading this book myself so I can TRULY get to know the person I admire so much. Thank you Ash. Honoured to call you my friend...

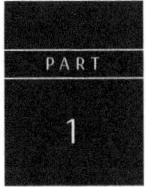

PART 1

Around the early part of 1996 as I turned twenty-three, my parents got pay TV. All of a sudden I was exposed to so many shows both old and new. One day I saw a wrestling show and it featured all the old classic wrestlers from the eighties that I was a fan of but had forgotten about, plus it was presented in a way that seemed almost realistic. I became interested in wrestling again and would watch WCW (World Championship Wrestling) weekly on a religious basis. I thought it was so cool that they had Hulk Hogan, Randy Savage and Ric Flair plus exciting new wrestlers who were a lot smaller in stature but showed a new athletic element to the sport. My new favorite was Chris Benoit as he reminded me of a smaller guy I had seen as part of the British Bulldogs, namely the Dynamite Kid. The resemblance in wrestling style was uncanny, so explosive and intense, and I would obsess over it during the next part of my life which was only six or so months away.

I was drinking a few times a week but on a day in late November I woke up to watch a wrestling pay-per-view at around 11am (time difference with USA). I don't know how but I decided to stop drinking and never take drugs again. I wanted my brain back. Wrestling might save me from being transgender and I might even become famous. I was excited and started lifting weights and studying wrestling in slow motion. Looking back I feel that I was just fooling myself as all I experienced for the next five years was daily pain and a further build-up of self-hatred.

My brother was a regular patron at "Stylus Nightclub" and he got talking to the exhibition boxing promoter there named Jim Demirov. My brother mentioned how much I was into wrestling and Jim gave him the number of a trainer for me, although he also stated it's a very tough industry and they don't let just anyone train. I got the number towards the end of the year and discovered that the trainer was a veteran wrestler from the old Festival Hall days named George "The Hitman" Julio.

In January of 1997, I rang the number that Jim Demirov had given to my brother to pass along to me. George picked up and I said I wanted to learn wrestling and he said to come and try it next Wednesday morning. I didn't realise it at the time but the pro-wrestling business in Australia was closed off to the general public. You couldn't just call up a school and pay to learn, which ironically is what it would turn into several years later. The business side of it was oosely controlled by elements of the Mafia and they would sometimes let people try out if they knew a contact, but most tryouts resulted in that person quitting.

I made the trek from Box Hill to George's home in Sunshine North via public transport which would take between two to three hours. I probably could have driven but I was still trying to cope with the PTSD of a serious car accident I had when I was twenty one. I hit the brakes while I lost control in the wet and of course, it made it much worse. I remember seeing cars only metres away from me and I saw my life flash before my eyes. The front passenger side was crushed right up to the middle of the car, if I have had a passenger they would have probably died and I would have gone to prison for drunk driving.

My head was split open and I was eventually taken to hospital smelling like a brewery. I think the police might have been on their way there too, and I knew if I had a blood test from the staff that I would be in big trouble. I asked a nurse if I could go to the toilet and she said "Yes but be quick to return". I snuck my way out of the hospital and walked home taking a bunch of back streets and parks. So I didn't get charged with drunk driving and had dodged another bullet so to speak. It gives me great shame to admit that it took another twenty or so years of drunk driving until I finally got caught. I estimate it to be in the thousands, I say that with absolute disgust and hatred and it is something I can never forgive myself for.

By the time I got a bus, two trains and walked forty-five minutes to George's training gym I had asthma so I needed to stop off at a park next to his house and inhale some Ventolin. I rang his doorbell and he let me in through his gate. "The Hitman" was shorter than me, probably in his early sixties, had muscles on muscles and looked like the real deal. I had trouble understanding his Maltese accent and he looked at my skinny little 57 kilogram frame and asked "So you want to be a wrestler?". Of course, I said and we both got into the wrestling ring.

He taught me the lock-up starting position which he referred to as the "referee hold". It took a few attempts to get it and we locked up as he pushed me onto the ring ropes. Holy shit I thought, these are not ropes. They are steel cables with garden hosing around them and it hurt like hell. He said "You ready?" and I nodded. Instantly he tripped me and my body slammed onto the canvas floor. My head hit the ring and I instantly realised how "real" professional wrestling was.

We kept training for about an hour with a lot of breaks.

I couldn't believe how hard it was. On TV it looked so easy, it looked like fun. The only way I can describe the athletic endurance needed would be if you played basketball and never stopped for a break, but kept falling hard over and over again and were not allowed to stop and rest. I thanked George and took my very sorry and aching body back home, with huge canvas burns on my elbows and I felt disappointed that all my aspirations since I was a kid were not going to come true.

Wrestling was as real as anything any top athlete goes through. It was being a stuntman going out to entertain an audience, but only having one take on each stunt as opposed to being filmed for television with multiple takes. I didn't return for about a month but when I called him again he agreed to give me one last chance. I found out years later that George only let me come back because I was honest with him in describing how hard it was, plus I think he saw that I had the heart for it.

When I returned for my next session I felt much more ready. I had been lifting weights at a local gym, running every day, practicing falls on my bed mattress and also mastering the referee hold (locking up) with my Dad. I had put on a few kilograms and as soon as George saw me he smiled and felt my trapezoid muscles. He probably also thought I was crazy because there were no sixty-kilogram wrestlers at all anywhere and he knew my body was going to feel the pain much worse than the bigger "real looking" wrestlers.

It took almost a full year of training for me to become ready for my first match in public. I was and have always been initially a slow learner at everything, but once it all clicks I excel very quickly. I was training at George's regularly and in the first few months he would torture me. I would scream in agony as he taught me the concept of real grappling: how to do it for real and how to imitate the same move without hurting your opponent. George told me about the honour of "kayfabe" which meant you never tip the public off that a wrestling match is an organised form of sports entertainment. It became a sacred oath to me but one that would be shat upon by others only a few years from then, thanks to WWE kingpin Vince McMahon.

As the months went by so too did my training schedule as it increased to twice a week for in-ring training, three times a week at my local gym and every Monday and Friday night taking adult gymnastics classes, then just before Christmas George gave me the news that I was ready and my first match would be next month against my new training partner Austen Young. I needed to organise my outfit and a wrestling name. It took a week or so to come up with my character "Cobra" and I thought it was a decent gimmick being so small, yet sneaky, quick and calculated.

It wasn't until I stepped into the dressing room at the Reggio Calabria Club in Brunswick on January 17th,

1998 that I finally realised the brotherhood and sisterhood of the industry. Psycho Kid Thunder and Ricky Diamond were chatting to each other and laughing about life. I had seen them wrestle a few times and it looked like they legitimately hated each other. Mario Milano was chatting with Con Iakavidis, Bully the Brawler and Wayne Starr.

I was introduced to every person in the room and shook their hand as requested by George. In the wrestling business you must shake hands very softly, because using a firm grip indicates that you are a rough worker and every wrestler wants to be assured that you are a light worker while putting their life in your hands. A "light worker" means that when you do any wrestling move your application against your opponent is so relaxed that you are barely connecting and it's up to your opponent to "sell" that move realistically. There are exceptions to this skill such as hitting in certain areas extremely hard that are deemed safe to do so like the upper back.

I had a chat with the commentary team of Peter Farry and "Mean" Gene Gatto. The promoter Sam Rossi introduced himself as we sat down to get dressed and warm up for the opening match of the evening. Austen and I had been practicing for a few months and had several "spots" worked out, but for the most part, every match back in those days was improvised, which hence was why I trained for almost a whole year. "Spots" are a series of combined moves that show off your individuality, character and signature finish. The winner of the match is pre-determined but if you think it's all just fake pantomime, I can assure you that it is as real as any high-contact sport.

The wrestling ring is similar to a boxing ring. The flooring is made up of several large boards that all link in together and sit above several steel beams, then covered with a piece of very thin foam or carpet, and topped off with a tightly fitted canvas mat. The ropes are industrial steel cables similar to electrical wires that hang between electricity poles, tightened up to make them springy and covered with rubber hosing. Underneath the ring is a huge spring in the middle that lets the floorboards move up and down slightly to somewhat lessen the impact when you fall.

I was extremely nervous as I walked out to the ring. The crowd laughed at how small I was at only 64 kilograms but my muscle tone was quite defined. I remember my first bump in the "real" ring and it felt like concrete. The training ring at George's had extra gym mats which made the impact more bearable, but the falls in this one were devastatingly painful. It's a ring made for people around the 90 kilogram mark not a tiny lightweight like me. The match went to plan: a time limit draw and we got booked again for the following show next month. I felt like I had no place in this industry, I just couldn't toughen up enough or improve at a steady rate. It would be hard to imagine that in just over a year I would be one of the top wrestlers in the country.

That next show in February I saw probably the greatest and purest hardcore match I had ever seen. It was so realistic I thought that Ricky Diamond and Psycho Kid Thunder were legitimately hurting each other. Over the following weeks I discovered that they were very good friends and around the same time I started training with Ricky Diamond, a second-generation young wrestler and a new high-flying lightweight called Chucky. They worked me relentlessly at Julio's gym and I think they were testing me to see how much heart I had and how badly I wanted it. When I look back now I honestly feel it was just another escape from reality, like drinking had been. I felt I was not worthy of being happy, so the dark side of my soul felt I deserved to be in pain, mental and physical, but under it all, I was an emotional wreck.

My next match was held at a new venue called the I.C.K.A Club in East Keilor against another new wrestler called Andy Wishbone. He was a very accomplished drummer in real life, playing in many of Melbourne's top bands over the years. His real name was George Kristy but within a couple of years, he would be one of the biggest stars in the industry as his flamboyant wise-cracking alter ego called "Screaming Lord Lush". We would often train together and call each other on the phone for a couple of hours chatting regularly. His wrestling skills were rather limited but when he got a hold of a microphone there was no one better. He was always cheery and as funny off-stage as he was on.

I felt such a deep sadness when I learned of his suicide in 2014 after he left the wrestling business in pursuit of becoming a famous musician. His band opened up for legendary guitar virtuoso Steve Vai while he toured Australia. He was an all-around great friend but hid his demons way too well for any of his friends to even suspect something was wrong. His story back in 1998 wasn't over by a long shot as he would be an integral contribution to the second wave of Australian wrestling (since the glory days of the 1970s at Festival Hall) which would see us perform several nights a week to regular crowds ranging from four hundred to well over a thousand patrons at every single event.

Once a month a group of us would travel up to Sydney to wrestle on a Sunday afternoon show. We would have shows on a Friday then Saturday night in Melbourne, get in and carpool for twelve hours and arrive in Sydney early morning. Do the afternoon show, carpool it back to Melbourne overnight and go to work on a Monday morning. This is where Ricky Diamond met Amy Action and they went out for the next six or so months. They formed Australia's first supergroup of villains called "The Cult" of which I was the last to join alongside Bulldog O'Reily and Screaming Lord Lush. Together we wreaked havoc on each show, running in to save each other and cheating when the referee was preoccupied. We were a gang that seemed to be somewhat of a highlight during each show and the crowds continued to build every week as the storylines became much more commercial.

Wrestling was going through a massive change overseas and we, the young and new wrestlers, were eagerly learning as much of the new hybrid of styles that we watched from pirated overseas video tapes. There was a divide in wrestling beginning to take shape. There were always the big muscle-bound monsters, but we smaller wrestlers began incorporating a faster pace influenced by lightweight athletes from Mexico and Japan. We were heading in new directions and the crowds were loving our efforts, often with us doing the stand-out matches of every event. With that came a lot more danger as we often flew over the top rope and landed on our opponents outside of the ring with no padding, only a cement or hardwood floor.

The internet was still in its early days and as I joined online forums I got to know two potential wrestlers from Adelaide who made videos doing crazy moves against each other in their backyards. Brett "Jag" Hartley-Jackson and Shannon "Havok" Mills became two great friends online and we would often exchange videos through the mail. Jag would eventually go on to become one of the top wrestlers in the world and became a trainer at the WWE about fifteen years later. I organised their first few matches in Melbourne and they were always technically miles ahead of anyone else on the show. They had found a trainer named Col Devaney and they set up their own wrestling company in South Australia which some of us Melbournians would bus over to fill in the card every month.

My first ever time at a nightclub was a result of being booked for a wrestling event called "Metromania" organized by Chucky and featuring Ricky Diamond, Amy Action, Bulldog O'Reilly and "Livewire" Johnny Parks, a Perth wrestler who had trained and wrestled in the United States. He was ripped and full of muscles and was the only participant who fitted the traditionally accepted image of what a wrestler is. I got a lift in with Bulldog and had pizza on Bourke Street before heading up to the Metro nightclub. It was going to be a very long and late night with matches planned hourly from midnight until four in the morning. I had to start work at nine so I was unsure how I would get through it all and hopefully not show up to work with any injuries like a black eye which had happened previously.

My match against Chucky was sometime after midnight and we went all out, throwing each other off the stage and onto the dance floor where patrons couldn't believe their eyes as we hit each other to the point of it being almost as real as any street fight. We also used a table outside of the ring and Chucky dived off the top rope and went through the table as I moved at the very last second. I came back after losing the match pretty sore but proud of what we had accomplished and the new precedent we had set for the Australian lightweight wrestling division.

The final match of the night was a Battle Royal, an event consisting of about ten of us in the ring at the same time, where being eliminated was done by being thrown over the top rope to the outside floor area. My old training partner Austen wanted to "juice" for this one but had never done it before so Ricky Diamond agreed to do it to him. The term "juice" means using a tiny piece of a razor blade and slicing it across your forehead to add more realism for the audience as blood trickles down across a wrestler's face. I never understood why wrestlers did that when the public, for the most part, thought it was fake blood anyway.

During the match, I was battling with various participants and I turned around to see Austen's face smothered in blood. It was pouring out and I was extremely concerned for him as Chucky and I arranged to get him out of the ring quickly for medical attention, all while making it look like he had been eliminated. The battle continued and somehow I ended up the winner of the lightweight title belt. It was Sherrie Sinatra's women's title belt that we borrowed but no one knew any different. I got cheered and booed equally and could tell the crowd wanted the big guy Johnny Parks to win and not a scrawny little high-flying newbie.

As I returned to the locker room backstage there was a paramedic tending to Austen. Ricky had accidentally juiced way too deep across the main artery at the top of the forehead. Blood was pouring out like a tap and Austen was looking extremely pale from the loss of blood. He was taken to the hospital and received a lot of stitches. I felt it a bit in poor taste that Chucky would sell VHS copies of the show with Austen's bloodied face as the main picture on the front cover but controversy sells and Chucky, who was never shy to offer an opinion, was quickly becoming rather unliked amongst the wrestling community. His brashness in the face of an industry that was run by older legends, combined with his young age, made him not well appreciated by the experienced wrestlers and promoters. I liked him though and we trained so often together that we became each other's favourite opponent.

My first concussion was received a couple of months later. I was booked to wrestle Austen on his first match back since the Metro incident. One "spot" involved him smashing my head into the turnbuckle and hanging on to my hair as he ran me head-first into the opposite turnbuckle. That was the plan but he ran and threw my head so hard and fast into the opposite turnbuckle that I completely missed it and went into the steel pole and blacked out for a second or two. I didn't know it at the time but it started a chain reaction of concussions over the next couple of years.

By this time I was signing autographs and was somewhat finally "famous" in the Australian wrestling world.

It felt great and I felt like an important person and even thought perhaps that my gender issues were fading away. The rest of the year saw me do a few more matches that climaxed at the "December to Remember" show where we hit a record crowd of around 800. It was "standing-room only" for more than half of the audience and we all had a feeling that wrestling was having its second coming since its gigantic following in the seventies. I said farewell to 1998 with an award as the "Australian Rookie of the Year". But that was only minor in comparison to where the next twelve months would take me.

My fitness level was becoming extremely high with only a few percent of body fat. Training every day became the norm for me whether it was in the ring, in the gym, gymnastics, or researching new moves and trying to understand the psychology of what makes a wrestler great as opposed to where I currently was. I hadn't sipped alcohol in about two years so there was a positive spin to all my inner torment of wishing I could be a woman. Looking back I would say that I just replaced an addiction to the booze with an addiction of self-harm through hurting my body. Nothing had changed inside me, it just became suppressed with the feeling of being a somewhat pseudo-celebrity in the wrestling world down under.

My last match at the "December to Remember" event was a real breakthrough and earned me a match in the main event at the first show of 1999. A tag-team match with Ricky Diamond against Chucky and the main superstar at the time, Psycho Kid Thunder. This was a difficult match due to my over-training. I had hurt a disc in my lower back and was seeing a local chiropractor twice a week. I was in serious pain during the entire match but took some strong codeine and anti-inflammatory tablets so I could at least get through it and take a few weeks off to recover. The next morning I could barely move and became bedridden for a few days but was fortunate enough to get time off from my job.

Training with the legend George "Hitman" Julio

The Cult, Aussie wrestling's first supergroup

Psycho Kid Thunder

Mean Gene & Peter Farry

Chucky -v- Cobra

Jungle Cat

Chucky powerbombing me on the hardwood pub floor

Moonsault off a couch

Ricky Diamond suplexing me through a table off the top

Chucky throwing me over a balcony

Cage match at the Epping Centre

Steve Frost, Tash, Extreme Dream Chucky, Adrian Manera, Stevie Cool, Mel, JT Robinson, Rohan, TNT Havok, Jag, Cobra, Man in Black, Adam Kember

Wrestlerage crew on tour in Adelaide

Pics Courtesy of Adam Kember

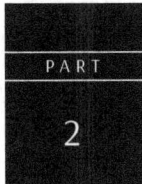

PART 2

April of 1999 was an evolving time as everything just started to come together and feel a lot more natural. We were doing two or three shows a week as well as Chucky setting up a series of new shows under the company name of JKW (Junior Kickstart Wrestling), featuring all young and more high-flying talent such as Ricky Diamond, Screaming Lord Lush, Man in Black, Bulldog O'Reilly, Psycho Kid Thunder, Skyhawk, Chucky's girlfriend and manager Tash, Austen Young, Blade Runner and myself.

There were a few important events around that time including my first "suicide dive" in a match against Blade Runner, which received a standing ovation. A suicide dive is where a wrestler runs fast across the ring and dives out onto their opponent who is outside the ring.

It would become my signature move, but also caused a lot of my injuries. My main memory of that match at the I.C.K.A Club was Screaming Lord Lush with "The Cult" running in to save me as Blade Runner was about to get the victory, and Lush kneeling to check how I was with the biggest grin on his face saying "Man you are crazy!". The next day Chucky had a show organised at the Queen Victoria Market. We both went through a table from the ring apron onto and breaking the table and hitting the cement ground. I remember Criss Fresh from a fan group called "The Asylum" proclaiming out loud: "There are people here laughing and saying it's not real, well have a look at that. Let's give them a round of applause". We had done something never done before in Australian wrestling, and although I was in tremendous pain, I loved that I was finally somewhat famous...well at least to Aussie wrestling fans!

A week or so later Chucky and I were the opening match for a new venue at the Macedonian Club in Epping. We had a few good spots planned out from our training session the night before at "The Dungeon" in Richmond. It was a martial arts gym where the owners allowed us to train up-and-coming wrestlers in the basics. The head trainer was Ricky Diamond but myself and Chucky were there nearly every other week to help. The match set a new standard for Australian lightweight wrestling with high-flying moves never seen before in our country. We even went a bit hardcore with Chucky suplexing me onto the hardwood floor and the use of chairs as weapons.

We had stolen the show again and the ego of both of us felt rather proud even though I was hurt quite badly.

Around the same time, Chucky had booked a few monthly shows under his promotion's banner of JKW at a venue called the High Ryder Saloon. It was a pub along King Street, which at the time was notorious for gangland violence including an incident with Jason Moran and Alphonse Gangitano. These were Friday night shows in front of a heavily intoxicated audience consisting of three to four matches followed by the latest American pay-per-view streamed on a big screen.

Chucky and I had now established a reputation as two of the best lightweight wrestlers in Melbourne and a feud had developed over many months preceding our two hardcore matches at the King Street venue. We were so believable that most fans thought we hated each other in real life but we were actually very close friends. The first match in late April almost destroyed me. It was a "Falls count anywhere in the pub" match, so we did our usual moves but out on the hardwood floor as opposed to the spring of the wrestling ring. After I took a powerbomb on the floor, I hit the back of my head and knew I was in deep shit. I continued through the pain and copped two suplexes again on the wooden floor, but I did manage to do a moonsault (backflip) from the back of a couch. I ended up unconscious and getting pinned on the pool table. Most of it was a blackout and although I was in horrible pain, I felt good about myself.

It was a feeling that "I am such a shit human being that I deserve this and I am prepared to die to void my inner emotional pain".

The re-match the following month, we introduced the use of barbed-wire in another hardcore match. Chucky brought along a folded-up chair wrapped in the wire and I used it to win the match by giving him a "Frankensteiner" from the top turnbuckle onto the chair. Again we took the match all around the pub and got near the exit where the crowd started chanting for us to go out onto King Street to fight. The owner Trevor blocked our path and unfortunately that was the last wrestling event ever held there. Trevor also ran a strip club upstairs and the guys would frequent it after the show. I felt ridiculously uncomfortable as the boys were turned on by the ladies while I secretly wanted to be a lady.

In July myself and Chucky caught a bus overnight to premiere our Melbourne wrestling style for the AWF (Australasian Wrestling Federation) at the Blacktown Civic Centre in Sydney. It was a new company started up by a wrestler called TNT (Greg Bownds) and a rather wealthy financier Rob Jones. Word had been getting around the wrestling industry in Australia about our previous matches and we didn't disappoint anyone as we had a match that would be later voted "Australian Match of the Year" by internet fans. I also got to meet a celebrity called Vulkan from the TV show "Gladiator" as he faced off against TNT in the main event later that night.

One of my favorite matches happened around that same month, again at the Macedonian Club in Epping for the NWA (National Wrestling Australia) promotion run by Jim Demirov. It was a semi-main event and was for the Hardcore Championship against title holder Ricky Diamond. He had a bunch of great spots planned and he even brought along the kitchen sink, literally. The end of the match had me getting suplexed from the top turnbuckle right through a table that ironically we had put together earlier that day with the help of my Dad. I even got paid a bonus of twenty dollars which brought my pay up to seventy dollars. I accidentally gave Ricky a concussion during the match by smashing his head with a frypan. I hit him so hard that the handle broke off.

The AWF called again with an offer I couldn't refuse. They would be touring the East Coast over a month with a show called "Psychotic Slam" featuring Australia's best wrestlers and international talents Super Dragon, Gothic Knight, Chris Candido with Sunny, Marty Janetty and Sabu. I could not believe my good fortune to be included as one of Australia's best and it took about one second to agree to such a privilege. OMG, I was becoming famous now and this tour would cement my position and future financial opportunities within the industry. I was twenty-six and famous, broke as a joke but I had accomplished something barely anyone in society could...I was fucking famous! Well, kind of...

A week before the AWF tour I had a very serious concussion. The JKW crew were booked in Adelaide, South Australia at the Thebarton Theatre for the first major wrestling show there in decades. It was a sold-out event with around 1,800 patrons selling at around the $40 mark per ticket. It was a tournament featuring myself, JT Robinson, MIB (Man in Black), Steve Frost, Chucky, Tash, and local talent Matt Rott, Larry Rhino, and Mad Max Miller who would later become one of Australia's finest actors, appearing in the TV shows "Home & Away", "Underbelly" and "Gallipoli" as well as movies such as "Wolf Creek", "Animal Kingdom" and "The Line". Also flown in was TNT from Sydney to fight Chucky in an extra non-tournament main event.

The majority of the crew from Melbourne had to take an overnight bus to Adelaide while Chucky managed to get a flight seeing that he had organised the event alongside the local promoter Adrian Manera. As we waited at the departure Greyhound bus depot, Chucky informed us that the previous week the venue in Adelaide had been shot up by the local Mafia in response to our event "invading" their city without a pay-off. In those days wrestling was somewhat governed by the Mob and Chucky was not well-liked, especially in a new location interstate.

When we arrived in the afternoon at the venue it looked huge and it was hard to believe it was sold out. The downside was the ring...it was a boxing ring with no spring under the floorboards and in a few hours it contributed to a concussion so bad that I would never fully recover. My first and only match of the JKW tournament was against JT Robinson from Sydney. I had been corresponding with him over the internet and he was instrumental in getting myself and Chucky booked for matches at the upcoming "Psychotic Slam" tour.

We had some great spots planned but my small athletic body was not ready for continuous bumps on a boxing ring. There was no give whatsoever and I received a few devastating knocks to the back of my head. The "show plan" was to have me eliminated by Chucky interfering in the match and later in the night challenge Chucky to a hardcore match for my revenge. I was too badly concussed to follow through with the original idea so the plans had to be altered. Jag drove me to a doctor's clinic but, upon seeing the dozens of people waiting, I decided to just go back to the dressing room at the venue and rest. It was by far the worst concussion out of many more to come, I truly felt as if a part of my brain was damaged that night. Yet I still had so much self-hatred that I felt I deserved it and in less than a week I would have to "man up" and go on tour with Australia's best and the incredible talents from America.

In August of 1999, we once again caught the overnight bus to Sydney and headed over to the AWF headquarters in Mount Druitt. We were pretty excited about being the only two Melbourne wrestlers to be asked to go on tour.

We were being accommodated for back in the city at the infamous Kings Cross at a five-star hotel called the "Park Royal". At around mid-afternoon the entire talent roster boarded a chartered bus to head to the first show in Newcastle. I couldn't believe it, suddenly I was on board with Sabu, Marty Janetty, Vulkan, Chris Candido, Sunny (aka. Tammy Lynn Sytch), Super Dragon, Gothic Knight, Jason Helton, TNT and others. Sabu suddenly lit up a joint and ended up arguing with the driver while Chris Candido and Sunny took over the onboard bathroom shooting up various substances. Marty Janetty and Vulkan kept joking with me calling me a "little Eddie Guererro" because of my mullet haircut, the same as Eddie's who was a world-class talent working in WCW at the time.

I sat next to Super Dragon (Danny Lyon) and we planned out our match for the night. I wasn't used to planning an entire match. All I had ever done was plan the start, a few "spots" and an ending while everything else was improvised on feel. The match had good potential to be a great high-flying opening bout, but I wasn't ready for the stiff style of Super Dragon. He was kicking me full-on and I was not ready for such a harsh beating. I always tried to work as light as possible while making it look realistic but barely touching my opponent. He was doing a shoot-type Japanese-influenced style and I came out of the match badly concussed again. I was so badly damaged in my head that I had to return home the following night. I was disappointed but I didn't know this was the beginning of my downward spiral from being one of the best in Australia to having constant injuries and potential brain damage. Chucky continued on the tour but I was seriously considering leaving the industry. I was just postponing the inevitable fact that my gender identity would have to be dealt with, yet it would take many more years to build up that type of courage.

Every match I had in the following year resulted in another concussion, some mild and some more serious. I decided in early 2000 that I would retire the Cobra character and go under a mask as a Mexican high-flyer called "Extremo Loco". It was a bit of a change to wrestle under a face mask but I wanted to make the character a mystery and was so inspired by the Mexican Lucha Libre style that I wanted to be one. I had some decent matches this time against Steve Frost, Jimmy Mustang and Bradman and it concluded with a semi-main event at the NWA Anniversary show in June against Chucky in a steel cage. The match won the Australian Match of the Year for 2000 but it was pretty ordinary in my opinion. The bars of the cage were brutal on my body and I was bruised for weeks afterwards. The finish had Chucky pinning me by giving me a powerbomb off the top turnbuckle onto a table covered in thumbtacks. I got an infection in my elbow from a tack getting lodged so deep it took a pair of pliers to remove it.

Again around August of that year, I was invited to perform at the annual AWF "Psychotic Slam" event but only for the Melbourne show as the opening match against Jimmy Mustang. I arrived at LaTrobe University for the event which also featured 2-Cold Scorpio, Psychosis, Blitzkrieg, Jason Helton, TNT, Psycho Kid Thunder, Lobo, Chucky and Con Iakavidis. I had begun drinking again and I showed up before the show after downing half a bottle of Port. It would prove to be a huge error as I went for my signature move in my match against Jimmy Mustang where I dived through the ropes onto my opponent on the outside of the ring. The last time I performed it as Cobra I broke my right hand but, this time as Extremo Loco, it would be my nose. I was meant to win the match but as soon as I smashed my face onto the hardwood floor I knew I was in serious trouble. I had my mask on and I instantly felt a warm sensation all over as blood began to pour out of my nose. It was a serious break and my nose was sideways on my face. I told Jimmy to just pin me as I couldn't continue. I had to be carried out of the ring by the referee.

Off to the Austin hospital it was, and I knew I was pretty

much done as a performer. Over the next couple of years I worked at the shows doing sound and even ended up working at Crown Casino for "All-Star Wrestling" as the sound and lighting director. I had a few more matches in a promotion called PCW (Professional Championship Wrestling) based out in Dandenong. It was a great time but my desire and hunger to be great had already vanished. At this time Lobo, Spike Steele, Johnny Rave and Mad Dog McCrea were becoming the finest wrestlers in Australia and two of them were about to get national press attention for an upcoming event called "Carnage" in September of 2002.

I remember chatting with Lobo and Mad Dog on the phone during the week prior as they discussed ideas for the match. They were about to create history with one of the most violent matches ever conceived in Australia. The ring ropes were removed and replaced with barbed wire. There were 40,000 thumbtacks on a bucket above the ring and set to be randomly dropped. The two fighters dipped their hands into super glue and their knuckles into a tray of broken glass. I was in the front row upon receiving a complimentary ticket as Mad Dog's guest.

It was one of the most disturbing matches I had ever seen. Similar matches were held regularly in Japan which I had watched on video, but to see it only meters away truly shocked me and I was concerned for my friends. Lobo "juiced" himself so deeply that it poured out of his forehead like a tap of running water. I was worried that he might lose consciousness from the loss of blood or even die. The crowd was stunned and some people were in shock. To be fair though, the audience was warned on multiple occasions that this would be extremely graphic. I honestly cannot put into words how far these two guys took it: to the next level and beyond. I was blown away and in disbelief at the amount of true pain they must have been in.

The media response the following week was extremely negative. It was a feature story on radio and television with interviews by Bulldog O'Reily and Gene Gatto. I think the main problem and why they spoke out was because PCW was an off-shoot of the traditional wrestling industry in Australia. Traditionally wrestlers and promoters had to go through a vetting system to see how badly they wanted to be involved and most failed. Ken Rock, owner of PCW, just created his own company without consulting with the decades-long veterans who controlled the industry. PCW had become hated by all other promotions but I saw the future in their athletes. They truly had become world-class performers and it was a shame that this match would cause them to close their doors for several years.

I knew it was time to move on. I had done too much permanent damage to my brain and body and any bump would now cause me a concussion. It was time to find another distraction that would help me block out the inevitable gender dysphoria issues that were building up and becoming stronger as each year passed.

I would occasionally go to a wrestling show to visit my friends including Chucky, Ricky Diamond, Bulldog, Mad Dog and the legend himself George Julio. Another friend that I was starting to follow quite closely was Matthew Muir, known as "Jungle Cat". When I was at my peak he was just starting and he certainly had "the look". He was ripped with muscles and went under a mask as a type of bodyguard for the bad guy manager Lord James Earl (Jim Demirov who was then also under a mask). He had been involved in matches here and there around 1999 and 2000, but when I saw him wrestling again around 2009 onwards, I was majorly impressed.

He was still respectful enough to honour the old-school way of improvisation with a few "spots" during his matches which impressed me greatly. Some wrestlers had gone down the way of planning their entire match, which ended up looking like a beautifully choreographed ballet, but Matt made it seem much more real. He had truly paid his dues and was now one of the top athletes in the industry down under. He had now removed the Jungle Cat mask which I thought was a clever move, but my gosh, his wrestling and in-ring character were easily worthy of a full-time career abroad. I would walk away from a show thinking he was the clear standout by far, even surpassing the more experienced, yet somewhat newer veterans like Ricky Diamond and Chucky.

I ended up having a falling out with Chucky when he borrowed about fifty of my VHS wrestling videos from the shows I had filmed, I tried to get them back but all he did was file a fraudulent intervention order claiming I was harassing him. It was honestly nothing more than him being upset because I started a website called "Aussie Wrestling Downloads" to sell digital versions of the shows I had filmed and owned the copyright to. He didn't like this because certain videos portrayed him in a bad light and I refused to remove them. He was always notorious for filing court orders against anyone portraying him in any type of not-so-flattering way.

I went to Sunshine Magistrates Court to fight the order but after a five-hour wait and three hours of driving through peak-hour traffic, I just couldn't be bothered ever returning to that shit-hole of an area again upon a proposed adjournment. Chucky didn't look healthy at all, his stomach made him look like he was "expecting" and he was a shell of the person I was once good friends with. I think that deep down he wasn't able to cope knowing that I was transgender and this was his way of never letting that part of me into his life. He had done this to multiple other people that he felt offended by. Making up some crap for a court order full well knowing there are no consequences for lying on an intervention order application. I agreed without any admission of guilt to the order, as long as I could still run my website but only post his matches that I was involved in. I thought that was a reasonable outcome and I was happy not to return to that area again. I still want my tapes back Chucky. I own the physical VHS cassettes and the intellectual property too as it was filmed on my camera... Jackass!

To read more about my life story please purchase a copy of my autobiography: **"BEYOND TRANS"**
ISBN: 9780975654613

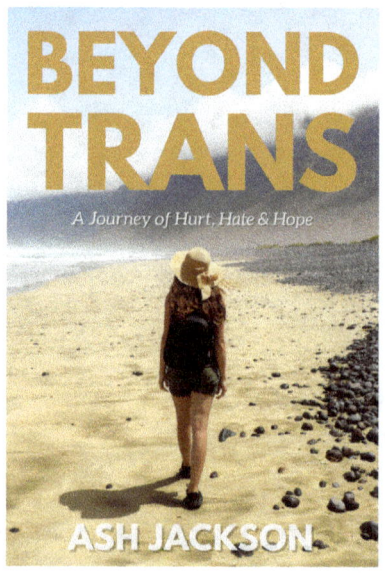

www.ingramcontent.com/pod-product-compliance
Lightning Source LLC
Chambersburg PA
CBHW072115290426
44110CB00014B/1920